EPIC Leader I

Advanced Discipleship Training

Dave Park, D.D. & The Infusion Team

His Passion Publishing

Infusion Ministries

2021

We highly recommend you watch the free leadership videos which accompany this material. You can find a link at the bottom of the 'EPIC Videos' page on our website at infusionnow.org.

First Printing: 2016
Current edition: 2021
Cover Design by Meghan Hamby
Interior designed and edited by Kristie Kroschel and the Infusion staff

Infusion Ministries is a national and international, interdenominational organization based in Knoxville, Tennessee. The purpose of Infusion Ministries is to awaken identity and establish freedom in the body of Christ. Our staff provides training and counseling through seminars, conferences, workshops, and resources with an emphasis on equipping pastors and small group leaders to do the same. We hope and pray that we will have the privilege to serve you and conduct one of our life-changing conferences or seminars for your group. Infusion Ministries is not a long-term counseling center. Through biblical truths and resources, we encourage and help believers in their walk with God.

Infusion Ministries
P.O.Box 22087
Knoxville, TN 37933
865-966-1153

infusionnow.org

CONTENTS

Forward

 Welcome to Infusion Ministries EPIC Leader 1 Training. This material is also included in *Stomping Out the Darkness, Busting Free, EPIC Identity, and EPIC Freedom.* This training is for pastors, youth pastors, children's ministers, small group leaders, counselors and other leaders who desire to set captives free. It's no secret that there is a lot of bondage in our churches today. In a survey conducted by Infusion, 70% of born again, believing young people said they have heard voices in their heads, like a subconscious dialogue going on in their mind. 30% have had a presence in their room that they identified as the enemy. Jesus has given us the responsibility to set captives free, but to do this, we need a clear and transferable plan of spiritual formation, a way to set captives free. This training will equip you with the biblical tools you need to awaken identity and establish freedom in your church.

We also have resources for other aspects of Christian living and ministry, for both youth and adults, on our website. Visit infusionnow.org or call 865-966-1153 to order by phone. If there is any way we can serve you, please let us know.

Blessings,

Dr. Dave Park

Thanks for leading others to the truth that will set them free!

> *"If you abide in my word, you are truly my disciples,*
> *and you will know the truth, and the truth will set you free."*
> *John 8:31-32*

What is Identity-Based Spiritual Formation?

Identity-based spiritual formation is a *grace-driven*, *position-in-Christ* oriented development process in which the soul grows in conformity to the image of Christ. This process seeks to balance all the needed spiritual approaches.

Grace-driven means that our spiritual formation is based on the freedom that we now have in Christ: the freedom to do what pleases Christ rather than doing what we have to do (legalism) or doing our flesh desires (license). Grace means we have both God's unmerited favor and even a freedom to fail as we grow into Christ-likeness.

Position-in-Christ oriented means our spiritual formation has, as its foundation, our identification with Christ in His crucifixion and resurrection (Romans 6:4, Galatians 2:20 and Colossians 3:4). Our old (sinful) life before we received Christ has been exchanged for the new (holy) life that we now have in Christ.

This identity-based spiritual formation approach moves us from a *works-based* acceptance to a *grace* oriented life, from legalism to liberty, because it centers on our acknowledgment that Christ's life is our life.

I please God.

In Luke 6:40 Jesus said, *"A disciple is not above his teacher, but everyone, when he is fully trained, will be like his teacher."* Our personal development involves training from the Holy Spirit and God's word, so we become like Christ, our teacher. Paul revealed in Romans 8:29-30 one of the most concise and clear intentions of the Lord for our spiritual formation: He foreknew, He predestined, He called, He justified, and He will glorify. We will become like Christ. Our souls will be conformed to the image of Christ.

· Discipleship is connecting people to Jesus.

Foundational Truths

These five foundational truths are the pillars of this balanced approach to spiritual formation.

1. The Sufficiency of the Scriptures (2 Timothy 3:16-17)

"All Scripture is breathed out by God and profitable for teaching, for reproof, for correction, and for training in righteousness, that the man of God may be complete, equipped for every good work..."

2. The Finished Work of Jesus (Colossians 1:27-2:10)

"To them God chose to make known how great among the Gentiles are the riches of the glory of this mystery, which is Christ in you, the hope of glory. Him we proclaim, warning everyone and teaching everyone with all wisdom, that we may present everyone mature in Christ. For this I toil, struggling with all his energy that he powerfully works within me. For I want you to know how great a struggle I have for you and for those at Laodicea and for all who have not seen me face to face, that their hearts may be encouraged, being knit together in love, to reach all the riches of full assurance of understanding and the knowledge of God's mystery, which is Christ, in whom are hidden all the treasures of wisdom and knowledge. I say this in order that no one may delude you with plausible arguments. For though I am absent in body, yet I am with you in spirit, rejoicing to see your good order and the firmness of your faith in Christ."

3. The Present Ministry of the Holy Spirit (John 16:7-15)

"Nevertheless, I tell you the truth: it is to your advantage that I go away, for if I do not go away, the Helper will not come to you. But if I go, I will send him to you. And when he comes, he will convict the world concerning sin and righteousness and judgment: concerning sin, because they do not believe in me; concerning righteousness, because I go to the Father, and you will see me no longer; concerning judgment, because the ruler of this world is judged. I still have many things to say to you, but you cannot bear them now. When the Spirit of truth comes, he will guide you into all the truth, for he will not speak on his own authority, but whatever he hears he will speak, and he will declare to you the things that are to come. He will glorify me, for he will take what is mine and declare it to you. All that the Father has is mine; therefore I said that he will take what is mine and declare it to you."

4. The Faith Response of the Disciple (Galatians 3:1-6)

"O foolish Galatians! Who has bewitched you? It was before your eyes that Jesus Christ was publicly portrayed as crucified. Let me ask you only this: Did you receive the Spirit by works of the law or by hearing with faith? Are you so foolish? Having begun by the Spirit, are you now being perfected by the flesh? Did you suffer so many things in vain—if indeed it was in vain? Does he who supplies the Spirit to you and works miracles among you do so by works of the law, or by hearing with faith- just as Abraham 'believed God, and it was counted to him as righteousness?'"

5. The Support of the Body of Christ (Hebrews 10:17-25)

"…then he adds, 'I will remember their sins and their lawless deeds no more.' Where there is forgiveness of these, there is no longer any offering for sin. Therefore, brothers, since we have confidence to enter the holy places by the blood of Jesus, by the new and living way that he opened for us through the curtain, that is, through his flesh, and since we have a great priest over the house of God, let us draw near with a true heart in full assurance of faith, with our hearts sprinkled clean from an evil conscience and our bodies washed with pure water. Let us hold fast the confession of our hope without wavering, for he who promised is faithful. And let us consider how to stir up one another to love and good works, not neglecting to meet together, as is the habit of some, but encouraging one another, and all the more as you see the Day drawing near."

For sin will have no dominion over you, since you are not under law but under grace (Romans 6:14).

But now we are released from the law, having died to that which held us captive, so that we serve in the new way of the Spirit and not in the old way of the written code (Romans 7:6).

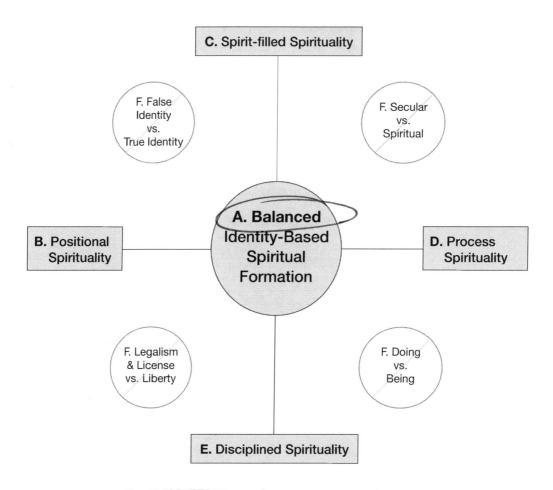

A. Identity-Based Spiritual Formation

Identity-based spiritual formation is a *grace-driven*, *position-in-Christ* oriented development process in which the soul grows in conformity to the image of Christ. This process seeks to balance all the needed spiritual approaches.

B. Positional Spirituality

Positional spirituality is an approach to the spiritual life based on a believer's position or identity in Christ. Identification with Christ in His crucifixion and resurrection (Romans 6:4, Galatians 2:20 and Colossians 3:4) means that our old life has been exchanged for the life of Christ. This approach moves us from a *works* based acceptance to a *grace* oriented life and from legalism to liberty because it centers on our understanding and internalization that Christ's life is our life.

Know your positional truth

C. Spirit-filled Spirituality — *Strong*

Spirit-filled spirituality is an approach that considers how to appropriate the leading and guidance of the Holy Spirit. The believer draws from the Spirit's love, wisdom, and power to live the spiritual life. This approach stresses the biblical implications of the Holy Spirit as a personal, present being rather than as a mere force.

D. Process Spirituality — *Sanctification*

Process spirituality considers what it means to be faithful to the process of life in Christ rather than being driven by perceived spiritual "successes" or "failures." It also focuses on abiding in Christ and practicing his presence. In our culture, we increasingly tend to be human "doings" rather than human "beings." The world tells us that what we achieve and accomplish determines who we are, but the Scriptures teach that who we are in Christ should be the basis for what we do. The dynamics of growth are inside out rather than outside in.

⑤ E. Disciplined Spirituality — *weak*

Disciplined spirituality stresses the benefits of these varied disciplines. There has been a resurgence of interest in the classical disciplines of the spiritual life. At the same time, it recognizes the needed balance between radical dependence on God and personal discipline as an expression of obedience and application.

F. Imbalanced Spirituality

False Identity Equations	vs.	True Identity in Christ
Secular	vs.	Spiritual
Doing	vs.	Being
Legalism and License	vs.	Liberty

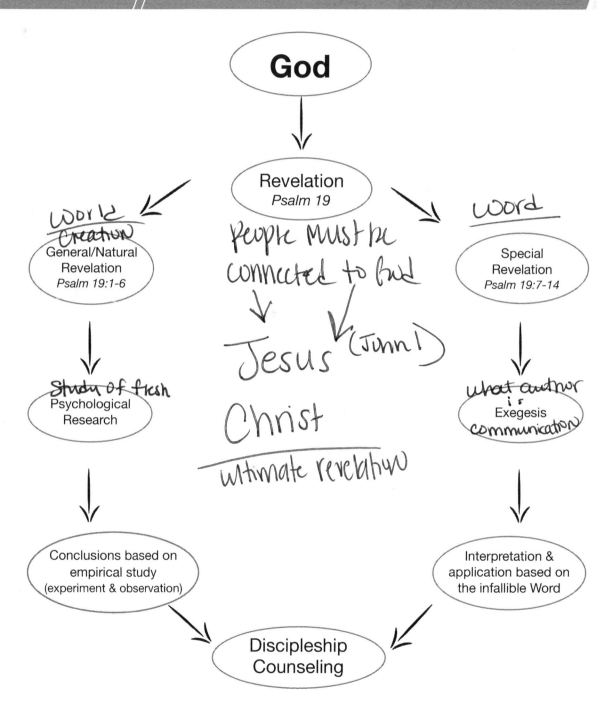

Adapted from Anderson, N.T. (2003) *Discipleship Counseling,* (p. 26). Ventura, CA: Regal Books.

Some Important Considerations

- The scientific method is valuable in describing what is observable through the five senses, but it cannot explain the supernatural or the mystery of the human heart and mind.

  - Neither God nor the devil will submit to our empirical study.

  - The physical sciences are by and large precise; the social sciences are not.

- General/Natural revelation must (always) be examined and explained in the light of special revelation (the Word of God).

  - Our understanding of the natural and supernatural world (apart from God's revelation of truth) will always be filtered through and colored by our grid of culture, education, and personal experience. *who is the filter? our background*

  - Methods of counseling borrowed from secular psychology (must) be brought under the scrutiny of the word of God (See Romans 12:9).

- A biblical approach to discipleship counseling must be based on the foundational truths listed on pages 6-7.

- The Holy Spirit (himself) effects personal liberation and transformation as (he) reveals, convicts, imparts new life, counsels, empowers, intercedes, and comforts (John 14:26; 16:7-15, 1 Corinthians 2:10-11, Ephesians 1:17-20, Romans 8:26-27, Galatians 5:22-25).

> God's Word reminds us to stay balanced, even in our spiritual walk and spiritual formation. Solomon said, "Do not be overrighteous, neither be overwise—why destroy yourself? Do not be overwicked, and do not be a fool — why die before your time? It is good to grasp the one and not let go of the other. Whoever fears God will avoid all extremes" (Ecclesiastes 7:16-18 NIV).

How are people struggling?

Introduce the gospel & salvation to them

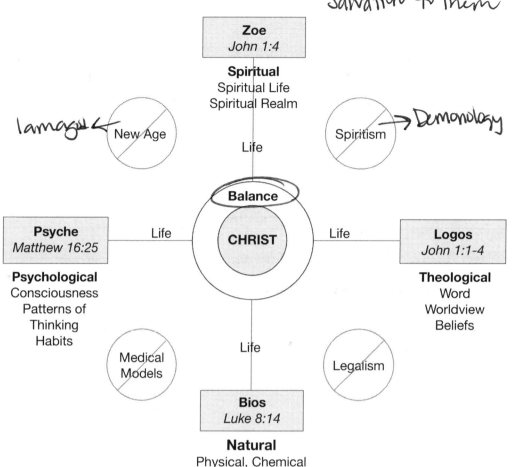

Zoe
John 1:4

Spiritual
Spiritual Life
Spiritual Realm

Iamage ← New Age

Spiritism → *Demonology*

Life

Balance

CHRIST

Life

Psyche
Matthew 16:25

Psychological
Consciousness
Patterns of
Thinking
Habits

Life

Medical Models

Legalism

Logos
John 1:1-4

Theological
Word
Worldview
Beliefs

Life

Bios
Luke 8:14

Natural
Physical, Chemical

Adapted from Anderson, N.T. (2003) *Discipleship Counseling,* (p. 37). Ventura, CA: Regal Books.

Mental illness vs. spiritual conflict

- Mental health is usually defined as being in touch with reality and relatively free from anxiety.

- Anyone caught in a spiritual conflict would fail on both counts!

- A biblical view of mental health begins with a true knowledge of God and a true knowledge of who we are as children of God.

- Those in spiritual bondage generally have been significantly deceived in both of these areas.

If a person doesn't have an understanding of Eph. 6 then you cannot go any further

Psychological vs. spiritual

- Spiritual conflicts (always) involve our mind, emotions, will, personality, developmental issues, etc.

- Psychological problems always involve the "spiritual" because God is omnipresent, the armor of God is always necessary, and temptation, accusation, and deception by the devil are constant realities.

    Avoid the two extremes:

    - Psychotherapeutic methods that ignore spiritual realities

    - Deliverance ministries that ignore personal development issues and bypass the counselee's responsibility

    The gospel and a biblical worldview need to be the framework of our counseling methods.

The Individual has to have the responsibility.

Spiritual conflict vs. demon possession (Ephesians 6:10-18)

- Seek to diffuse the controversy in the church through differentiating between demonic "ownership" (which can never happen to a believer) and demonic "influence" and "control" (which can and does).

- The church must take responsibility for helping people in bondage and not take a "head-in-the-sand" approach to spiritual conflict.

Truth encounter vs. power encounter (2 Timothy 2:24-26)

- Our approach to dealing with spiritual conflict must come from the epistles, not the gospels.

- Counselees must assume responsibility for their own health and freedom.

> ***Etymology*** deals with the meaning of a word by analyzing its elements, considering its root and derivation. When we look at the word for demonization, improperly translated "demon possession," it is more clearly understood as demonic control of a somewhat passive human, (daimonizomai) rather than "possession" and "oppression." We should refer to this control as demonization, or demonic influence.

Introduction

James 3:1 warns us: *"Not many of you should become teachers, my brothers, for you know that we who teach will be judged with greater strictness."*

Those are sobering words that every discipler should take to heart. The Lord Jesus pronounced a stern judgment upon anyone who would cause *"one of these little ones who believe in me to sin, it would be better for him to have a great millstone fastened around his neck and to be drowned in the depth of the sea"* (Matthew 18:6).

People are often very impressionable and highly vulnerable to the influence of a spiritual leader. Many will practically hang on every word you say and everything you do because you represent a source of love and acceptance they never experienced before they knew Christ. We dare not use this attention and admiration as a means of stroking our fragile egos. We are called, like Jesus, to serve and not be served. Therefore, it is essential that we develop the kind of character and lifestyle that points those we disciple to dependence upon the Lord Jesus Christ.

The Pursuit of Godly Character (2 Peter 1:3-11)

³ His divine power has granted to us all things that pertain to life and godliness, through the knowledge of him who called us to his own glory and excellence, ⁴ by which he has granted to us his precious and very great promises, so that through them you may become partakers of the divine nature, having escaped from the corruption that is in the world because of sinful desire.

past tense

⁵ For this very reason, make every effort to supplement your faith with virtue, and virtue with knowledge, ⁶ and knowledge with self-control, and self-control with steadfastness, and steadfastness with godliness, ⁷ and godliness with brotherly affection, and brotherly affection with love, ⁸ For if these qualities are yours and are increasing, they keep you from being ineffective or unfruitful in the knowledge of our Lord Jesus Christ. ⁹ For whoever lacks these qualities is so nearsighted that he is blind, having forgotten that he was cleansed from his former sins.

Always Increase
Always Sharpen

¹⁰ Therefore, brothers, be all the more diligent to confirm your calling and election, for if you practice these qualities you will never fall. ¹¹ For in this way there will be richly provided for you an entrance into the eternal kingdom of our Lord and Savior Jesus Christ.

God has given us everything we need for life and godliness (v. 3).

We are partakers of the divine nature (v. 4).

Our responsibility is to do everything necessary to add to our faith (vv. 5-7):

    Virtue (moral excellence)
    — Knowledge —
    — Self-control —
    Steadfastness
    Godliness
    Brotherly affection
    Love

Have a plan... Make a list... work on it daily

Having these qualities and growing in them is the key to a useful and fruitful life (v. 8).

Knowing (or not knowing!) who you are, determines what you do (or don't do!) (v. 9).

A sure walk and a warm welcome (vv. 10,11)

Connected to the Hub

Spokes without the Hub

We live in a very task-oriented society. People in trouble usually cry out, "What must I do?" The implication is that if we just stopped behaving one way and started behaving another way, we'd be all right.

Hundreds of good Christian books have been written on every conceivable aspect of life: dating, marriage and parenting, divorce and remarriage, work and play, and back again. But how are we doing? Are we as a church making significant strides ahead in these areas?

Many believers have simply put Jesus in a compartment of their life, they call upon Him when He is needed, but He is not in control of their everyday personal life. They rely on their own strength to manage life's issues.

A Compartmentalized Life

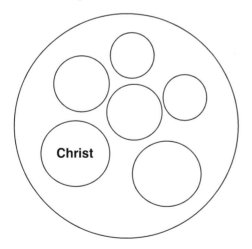

A Christ Centered Life

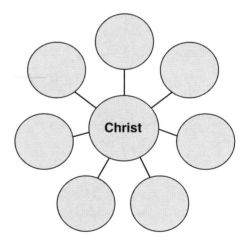

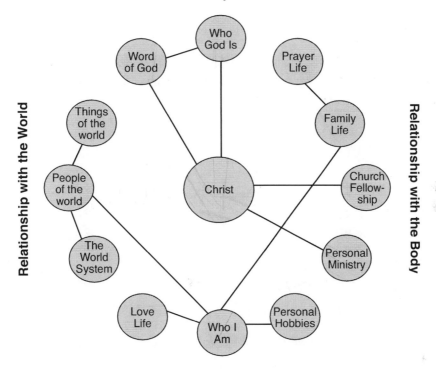

Relationship with God

Relationship with the World

Relationship with the Body

Relationship with the Self

> Perhaps, in many cases, we have done a good job of identifying and teaching the spokes of the wheel, but have failed to connect every aspect of life, and relationships to the hub!

Getting Connected to Christ

Our first objective in life must always be to know Christ in us, the hope of glory (Colossians 1:27). We have to teach people to abide in Christ, or they will never grow and bear fruit. We have to be first rooted in Him in order to walk in Him. If we reverse the order, we can fall into the trap of a subtle form of "positive legalism" – believing we are spiritual because we follow a list of correct behaviors.

We must first connect people with God. Only He can grant repentance; only He can give life, and only He can enable us to live a victorious life. Trying to help people establish their identity, find their purpose in life, enjoy meaningful relationships, and have their needs met *apart* from Christ is precisely the devil's agenda on planet earth!

You Reproduce According to Your Kind

Are your life and ministry genuinely connected to the Hub, the Lord Jesus Christ, or are you operating out of the energy of the flesh, masquerading cleverly as spirituality?

The person you are discipling will pick up on it if you're not abiding in Christ and may drop out, give up, or worse; they may become like you. The following inventory is designed to shed light on this crucial issue.

Personal Walk and Ministry Inventory   *Good for Leadership*

- ‣ Am I growing in my heartfelt commitment to prayer, or am I getting so busy that prayer seems to be getting more crowded out and hurried?

- ‣ Am I experiencing an increasing love for people and other leaders I interact with, or do I find myself becoming increasingly impatient with them?

- ‣ Do I enjoy what I'm doing, or is it a struggle to just get out there?

- ‣ Do I struggle with the compelling need to prove to people in my ministry that I am doing a good job?

- ‣ Do I talk about numbers a lot (small groups, church attendance, salvations, etc.)?

- ‣ Am I able to leave work/ministry when I get home and on my day off, or do I always seem to find just one more thing to do?

- ‣ Am I cultivating hobbies and relationships apart from work/ministry, which I find refreshing and stimulating?

- ‣ Do I look forward to reading God's Word and being in my Father's presence, letting Him love me and guide me, or am I just going through the motions?

- ‣ Do others see a lifestyle of gratitude and praise to God, or would I be described as a grumbler, complainer, or worrier?

- ‣ Do I welcome the counsel of others (including my spouse), or do I come across as a defensive, slow-to-listen know-it-all?

- ‣ Am I struggling with sinful habits I can't break, or am I free?

• Do I have balance?
• Do I have boundaries?

Walking According to the Spirit (Galatians 5:16-18)

Not License

License: An excessive or undisciplined freedom resulting in an increasing compromise and tolerance for sin

Licentious: Lacking moral discipline, having no regard for accepted rules or regulations, with no fear of God

Relationship with God

Relationship with the World

Relationship with the Body

- Who God is
- Prayer Life
- Word of God
- Family Life
- Things of the world
- Christ
- Church Fellowship
- People of the world
- Personal Ministry
- The World System
- Personal Hobbies
- Love Life
- Who I am

Relationship with the Self

Not Legalism

The Law is a curse (Galatians 3:10-13)

The Law is powerless to give life (Romans 8:3, Galatians 3:21)

The Law stimulates the flesh (Romans 7)

> *"In returning and rest you shall be saved;*
> *in quietness and in trust shall be your strength."*
> (Isaiah 30:15)

Liberty (Galatians 5:1,13)

We are *"ministers of a new covenant, not of the letter but of the Spirit. For the letter kills, but the Spirit gives life"*

"Now the Lord is the Spirit, and where the Spirit of the Lord is, there is freedom" (2 Corinthians 3:6,17)

A Walk of Faith (Colossians 2:6)

Don't sit (passivity)

Don't run (endless, exhausting activity)

Illustrated in Mathew 11:28-30

Being Led by the Shepherd and the Spirit

"My sheep hear My voice, and I know them, and they follow Me" (John 10:27)

"For all who are led by the Spirit of God, these are sons of God" (Romans 8:14)

Lost / not born again

FLESH
(Romans 8:5-8)
Though the flesh can mean the body, it is the learned independence which gives sin its opportunity. The natural person who tries to find purpose and meaning in life independently of God is going to struggle with inferiority, insecurity, inadequacy, guilt, worry and doubts.

BODY
Tension or migraine headaches, nervous stomach, hives, skin rashes, allergies, asthma, some arthritis, spastic colon, heart palpitations, respiratory ailments, etc.

MIND
Obsessive thoughts, fantasy, etc

EMOTIONS
Bitterness, anxiety, depression, etc.

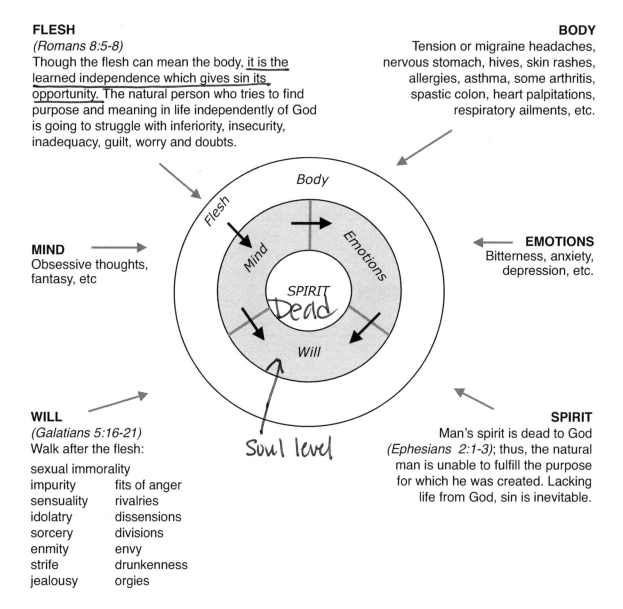

Body
Flesh
Mind
Emotions
SPIRIT *Dead*
Will

Soul level

WILL
(Galatians 5:16-21)
Walk after the flesh:

sexual immorality

impurity	fits of anger
sensuality	rivalries
idolatry	dissensions
sorcery	divisions
enmity	envy
strife	drunkenness
jealousy	orgies

SPIRIT
Man's spirit is dead to God *(Ephesians 2:1-3)*; thus, the natural man is unable to fulfill the purpose for which he was created. Lacking life from God, sin is inevitable.

THE SPIRITUAL PERSON
LIFE "IN THE SPIRIT" - 1 CORINTHIANS 2:15

FLESH
(Galatians 5:24, Colossians 3:5)
Crucifying the flesh is the believer's responsibility, on a day-by-day basis as he considers himself dead to sin.

BODY
Temple of God
(1 Corinthians 6:19-20)
Presented as a living and holy sacrifice *(Romans 12:1)*

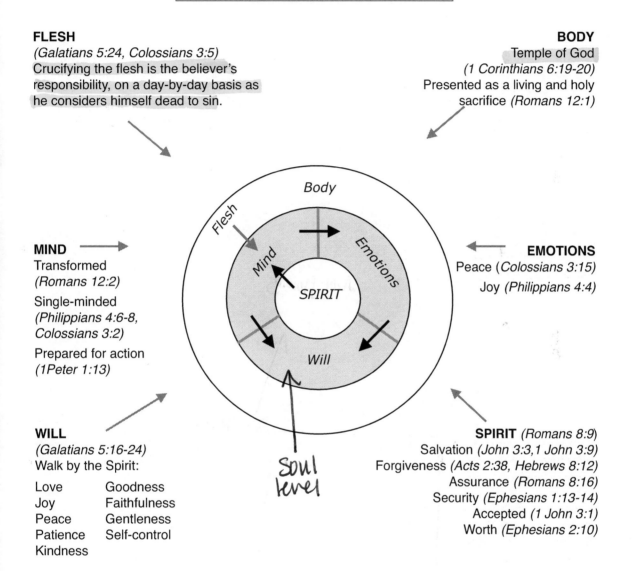

MIND
Transformed
(Romans 12:2)

Single-minded
(Philippians 4:6-8, Colossians 3:2)

Prepared for action
(1Peter 1:13)

EMOTIONS
Peace *(Colossians 3:15)*
Joy *(Philippians 4:4)*

WILL
(Galatians 5:16-24)
Walk by the Spirit:

Love	Goodness
Joy	Faithfulness
Peace	Gentleness
Patience	Self-control
Kindness	

Soul level

SPIRIT *(Romans 8:9)*
Salvation *(John 3:3,1 John 3:9)*
Forgiveness *(Acts 2:38, Hebrews 8:12)*
Assurance *(Romans 8:16)*
Security *(Ephesians 1:13-14)*
Accepted *(1 John 3:1)*
Worth *(Ephesians 2:10)*

THE FLESHLY PERSON
LIFE "ACCORDING TO THE FLESH" - 1 CORINTHIANS 3:3

FLESH *(Romans 8:5)*
The ingrained habit patterns still appeal to the mind to live independently of God.

BODY
Tension or migraine headaches, nervous stomach, hives, skin rashes, allergies, asthma, some arthritis, spastic colon, heart palpitations, respiratory ailments, etc.

MIND
Double minded

EMOTIONS
Unstable

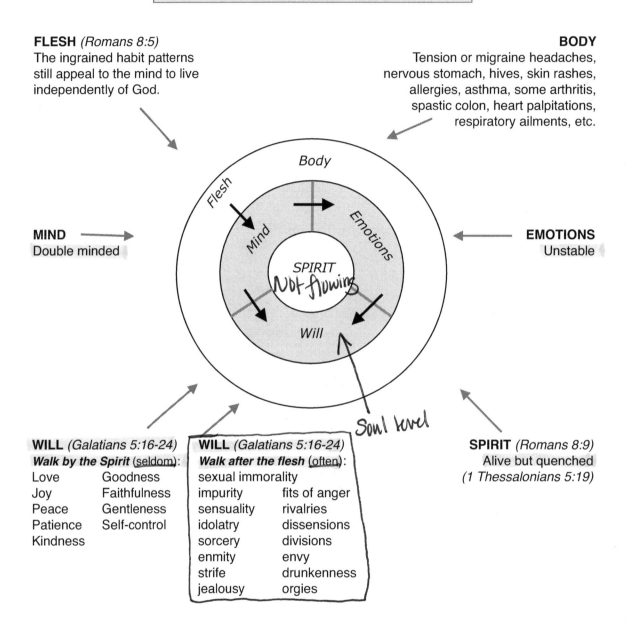

Body

Flesh

Mind

Emotions

SPIRIT
Not flowing

Will

Soul level

WILL *(Galatians 5:16-24)*
Walk by the Spirit (seldom):

Love	Goodness
Joy	Faithfulness
Peace	Gentleness
Patience	Self-control
Kindness	

WILL *(Galatians 5:16-24)*
Walk after the flesh (often):

sexual immorality	
impurity	fits of anger
sensuality	rivalries
idolatry	dissensions
sorcery	divisions
enmity	envy
strife	drunkenness
jealousy	orgies

SPIRIT *(Romans 8:9)*
Alive but quenched
(1 Thessalonians 5:19)

The Spirit's manifestations are manifold, but the New Testament distinguishes two primary ways in which believers can be filled with the Spirit.

The Inward Work of:	The Outward Work of:
Filling: *pleroo* and *pleres*	Filling: *pimplemi*
A growing state of being	A temporary experience
Produces character and wisdom	Empowers for ministry and service
The fruit of the Spirit	The gifts of the Spirit
The Spirit within	The Spirit upon
Purity	Power
Maturity	Manifestations
Becoming	Acting

The *inward work of the Spirit* produces Christ-like character and spiritual maturity.

The Greek verb *pleroo* and its cognate *pleres* refer to filling as a growing state of being.

These words are used of spiritually mature believers like Stephen and Barnabas, who are controlled by the Spirit (Luke 4:1-2, Acts 6:3; 7:55; 11:24; 13:52, Ephesians 5:18-19).

The *outward work of the Spirit* concerns divine empowerment for ministry and service.

The Greek verb *pimplemi* refers to filling as a temporary experience of the sovereign power of God that is evident in action.

This word is used for specific manifestations of the Holy Spirit in the lives of people like Elizabeth, Peter, and Saul (see Luke 1:41-42; 67, Acts 2:4; 4:8,31; 9:17-20; 13:9-10).

Hearing the Story

Sanctification Process

The apostle Paul revealed the essence of his discipleship ministry and identity based spiritual formation in Colossians 1:28-29 when he wrote:

"Him we proclaim, warning everyone and teaching everyone with all wisdom, that we may present everyone mature in Christ. For this I toil, struggling with all his energy that he powerfully works within me."

Levels of Spiritual Formation

Complete

Level One: You have been filled in Him (Col. 2:10).

Level Two: Rooted and built up in Him and established in the faith (Col. 2:7).

Leader → ***Level Three***: Having received Christ Jesus the Lord, so walk in Him (Col. 2:6).

Romans 6:3-10	*Knowing*
Romans 6:11	*Being*
Romans 6:12-14	*Doing*

If people are secure in their identity in Christ and are developing a mature Christian character, your discipling and counseling will be at level three. This level is basically "wisdom counseling," applying sound biblical principles to the problems of life. A small part of discipleship and counseling will occur at this level, but the vast majority of discipleship and counseling will be at level one or two.

Belief
Identity

Feelings

In the spiritual formation process, the problem presented will seldom be the whole (or real) issue. A barren, fruitless life indicates a faulty root (belief) system. The disciple can only reveal these underlying conflicts. The crucial variable will be whether the disciple perceives the discipler as the kind of person they can trust.

Since the problem or bondage presented is seldom the whole or real issue, we need to ask questions that reveal the root problems. Ask questions such as:

How did they come to Christ?

What do they believe about Jesus and the Bible?

Who has hurt them?

Have they ever been rejected?

What fear is present in their life?

In what ways have they walked away from God?

Have they misused their body sexually or abused drugs?

What negative habits do they have?

BARREN LIFE

Rejection

Rebellion

Fear

Unforgiveness   False Belief System

Be Aware of Fleshly Defense Mechanisms (1 John 1:5-2:2)

Our goal is to help the disciple walk in the light and enjoy fellowship with God and others. "Walking in the light" is not sinlessness; it is living a life of openness and honesty before God and men. It is owning up to our sin and trusting in Christ as our only defense (I Peter 2:23).

Trusting in fleshly survival techniques (defense, coping mechanisms), rather than in Christ, will yield the following behaviors:

Denial of reality: an attempt to protect ourselves by refusing to believe or face painful circumstances

- Avoidance – a conscious refusal to deal with real issues
- Suppression – a conscious denial of a problem by pushing down inside any surfacing emotions and attempting to live as if nothing was wrong (Psalm 32)
- Repression – an unconscious denial.

Fantasy: escaping from the real world and painful problems by entering into a world of imaginary achievement or counterfeit reality through daydreaming, TV, movies, books, video games, drugs, etc. (2 Corinthians 10:5, I Peter 1:13) Social Media, Internet

Identification: feeling better about yourself by associating with people or groups that are well-respected (1 Corinthians 3:4-5)

Reaction formation: a frantic effort to prevent one's dangerous desires from surfacing by vigorously opposing those desires in word and deed (e.g., someone addicted to pornography campaigning against it) (Romans 2:1)

Emotional insulation: withdrawal into passivity and from people in order to shield oneself from hurt and rejection (2 Corinthians 6:11-13)

Isolation: failure to recognize the whole situation in order to live only the part that is good (John 4:16-19)

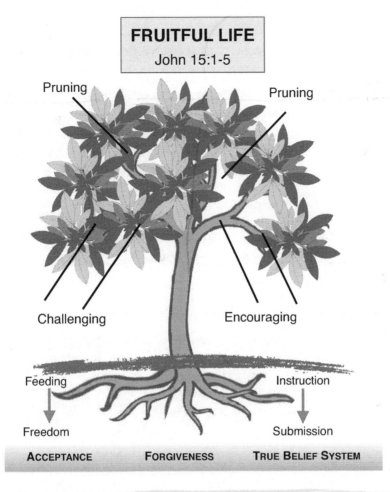

FRUITFUL LIFE
John 15:1-5

Pruning

Pruning

Challenging

Encouraging

Feeding

Instruction

Freedom

Submission

ACCEPTANCE   FORGIVENESS   TRUE BELIEF SYSTEM

Regression: retreating to earlier development levels involving happier times requiring less mature responses (Josh 7:7)

Displacement: taking out "pent-up" feelings (usually hostility) on objects or people less threatening than those which aroused them

Compensation: trying to make up for weaknesses by emphasizing one's desirable traits or trying to make up for frustration in one area by seeking gratification in another (Matthew 19:16-17)

Projection: placing the blame for difficulties upon others or blaming others for one's own character flaws (Luke 10:28-29)

Rationalization: atempting to prove that one's own immoral or unethical behavior is rational, justifiable, and deserving of approval (Luke 18:10-14)

Most people do not spend their time analyzing how they feel and why they feel that way. Most would rather bury themselves in activities rather than deal with their pain. Therefore, in complete dependence upon the Holy Spirit, the discipler must first help people assume responsibility for their attitudes and actions, and help them make plans for a future direction in line with God's will. Living responsibly as a child of God will involve living in harmony with family, church, friends, etc. *Community*

Constructing a new beginning for a disciple requires a realistic assessment of what is and what can be. Making unrealistic plans or presuming upon God is only setting the disciple up for failure and discouragement.

Differentiating between goals and desires is crucial since some things are beyond our right or ability or control. The "serenity prayer" expresses the attitude we should have:

> God, grant me the serenity to accept the things I cannot change,
>
> the courage to change the *things* I can, and the wisdom to know the difference.

We must also realize that most people do not spend their time analyzing how they feel and why they feel that way. Most would rather bury themselves in activities rather than deal with the pain. An attitude on the part of the discipler of complete dependence upon the Holy Spirit is essential.

Prerequisites (Proverbs 18:13)

If you had to confide in someone and tell them your deepest, darkest secrets, what character qualities would you want to see in that person?

Will you commit yourself to depend on God to make you that kind of person?

Process (Proverbs 20:5)

Listening (to both verbal and nonverbal clues)

- Experience: What has happened or is presently happening to them?

- Behavior: What did they do? What are they doing or not doing?

- Emotions: How do they presently feel about it?

Confronting

Clarifying their belief system and their identity in Christ by showing them the truth of God's Word.

- Leading them in renunciations of all lies they have believed, thus canceling all ground that the enemy has gained in their lives.

- Guiding them in repentance of all ungodly behavior and helping them know God's complete forgiveness.

- Encouraging them to forgive others from the heart.

An Ongoing Ministry

The counseling or teaching process is just the beginning. For people to walk in their freedom in Christ and grow into mature believers, they must be nurtured through ongoing discipleship and identity-based spiritual formation.

Do everything within your power to plug the people you disciple and counsel into such an environment. Pray for them, reminding them that they are responsible for seeking out and attending opportunities to continue to grow in Christ.

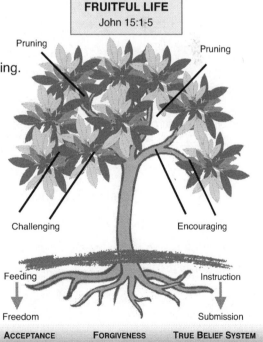

FRUITFUL LIFE
John 15:1-5

Pruning
Pruning
Challenging
Encouraging
Feeding
Instruction
Freedom
Submission
ACCEPTANCE   FORGIVENESS   TRUE BELIEF SYSTEM

"Therefore, as you received Christ Jesus the Lord, so walk in him, rooted and built up in him and established in the faith, just as you were taught, abounding in thanksgiving" (Colossians 2:6-7).

Since I Am In Christ

- I am now acceptable to God (justified) and completely forgiven. I live at peace with Him (Romans 5:1).

- The sinful person I used to be died with Christ, and sin no longer rules my life (Romans 6:1-7).

- I am free from the punishment (condemnation) my sin deserves (Romans 8:1).

- I have been placed into Christ by God's doing (1 Corinthians 1:30).

- I have received God's Spirit into my life. I can recognize the blessings He has given me (1 Corinthians 2:12).

- I have been given the mind of Christ. He gives me wisdom to make right choices (1 Corinthians 2:16).

- I have been bought with a price; I am not my own; I belong to God (1 Corinthians 6:19-20).

- I am God's possession, chosen and secure (sealed) in Him; I have been given the Holy Spirit as a promise of my inheritance to come (2 Corinthians 1:21-22, Ephesians 1:13-14).

- Since I have died, I no longer live for myself, but for Christ (2 Corinthians 5:14-15).

- I have been made acceptable to God (righteous) (2 Corinthians 5:21).

- I have been blessed with every spiritual blessing (Ephesians 1:3).

- I was chosen in Christ to be holy before the world was created. I am without blame before Him (Ephesians 1:4).

- I was chosen by God (predestined) to be adopted as His child (Ephesians 1:5).

- I have been bought out of slavery to sin (redeemed) and forgiven (Ephesians 1:6,7).

- I have received His generous grace (Ephesians 1:7-8).

- I have been made spiritually alive just as Christ is alive (Ephesians 2:5).

- I have been raised up and seated with Christ in heaven (Ephesians 2:6).

- I have direct access to God through the Spirit (Ephesians 2:18).

- I may approach God with boldness, freedom, and confidence (Ephesians 3:12).

Anderson, N. T., & Park, D. (2007) Since I Am In Christ in *Stomping out the Darkness (pp. 34-36). Bloomington MN: Bethany House Publishers.*

Truth Encounter

Many Christians who disciple and counsel people understand deliverance as being accomplished by an outside agent. The pastor/counselor calls up the demons in the victim, and, sometimes, tries to determine their rank and grounds to cast them out.

We refer to that method as the power encounter. This method often bypasses the issues that have caused the person to be in bondage in the first place. Many times, it fails to demonstrate the counselee's own authority in Christ, leaving them spiritually dependent on the discipler or counselor.

Teach ppl their authority

The power encounter method is derived primarily from the gospels, tradition, and experience. Before the cross, it would take an outside agent with specially endowed authority, such as Christ or the Apostles, to cast out a demon (for example, see Luke 9:1). After the defeat of Satan at the cross, Jesus said, *"all authority has been given to Me in heaven and upon the earth"* (Matthew 28:18-20). Every believer, regardless of their age, shares that authority as they are walking obediently and filled with His Spirit.

> It is no longer the responsibility of some ecclesiastical authority. It isn't what the *discipler or counselor* believes, confesses, forsakes, renounces, or whom the *discipler or counselor* forgives that counts. It is what the *disciple or counselee* believes and does that matters because that is every believer's responsibility.

et God eal w/ them. You are NOT the Holy Spirit.

All we can do is act as a facilitator. We refer to this method as the "truth encounter." This method requires you to work with the whole person, never bypassing their mind or assuming their responsibility. It also requires God to be involved as the central figure in the process. There is a very definitive passage in the pastoral epistles instructing us what to do. Take a look at 2 Timothy 2:24-26 on the next page.

"And the Lord's servant must not be quarrelsome but kind to everyone, able to teach, patiently enduring evil, correcting his opponents with gentleness. God may perhaps grant them repentance leading to a knowledge of the truth, and they may come to their senses and escape from the snare of the devil, after being captured by him to do his will" (2 Timothy 2:24-26).

Lord's servant: You must be dependent upon the Lord

Not quarrelsome: Don't get into useless dialogue

Kind: Compassion is the essential prerequisite

Able to teach: You have to know the biblical truth

Patience: Some counseling sessions may require more than 50 minutes

Gentleness: Don't get ahead of God's timing or lose control

God may perhaps: Only God can grant repentance.

History Taking

(See Sample "*Confidential Personal Inventory*" in the Appendix)

Family History

- Spiritual/Religious background
- Parent's marital relationship and home environment
- Health: genetic
- Generational sins (Exodus 20:4-6)

Personal

- Physical: rest, exercise, diet, sleeping (nightmares), medications
- Mental: what are they doing, thinking, watching, reading
- Emotional: depression, fear, anxiety
- Spiritual: salvation, assurance, fellowship

Determine Beliefs About God

(2 Corinthians 10:5, 1 John 4:1-10)

Proper View of God:	Truth about God is filtered through the grid of:	Improper View of God:
Loving, caring	1.Ignorance	Hateful and unconcerned
Good and merciful	2. False prophets and teachers	Mean and unforgiving
Steadfast and reliable	3. Disrespectful thoughts against God	Unpredictable and untrustworthy
Unconditional love and grace	4. Unhealthy interpersonal relationships during the early developmental years *Your earthly Father*	Conditional approval
Present and available		Absent when needed
Giver of good gifts	5. Role model of authority figures - especially parents	Takes away, "joy killer"
Nurturing and affirming		Critical and unappeasable
Accepting		Rejecting
Just, fair and impartial		Unjust, unfair, partial

Adapted from Anderson, N.T. (2003) *Discipleship Counseling,* (p.186). Ventura, CA: Regal Books.

*Chapter 1 of The EPIC Journey - The Lord's Prayer Journey deals specifically with our beliefs and view of God as Father.

Determine Beliefs About Themselves

• Do they fear a mental breakdown or insanity?

• Do they feel unloved, worthless, and rejected? (20% of Christians we surveyed have frequently had thoughts of suicide).

• Do they believe they are different than others? (over 70% of those we surveyed believe Christianity works for others but not for them).

Given truth to resolve their conflicts.

Note: There is a real line between God's responsibility and ours. On one side is God's responsibility. If we try to do for Him what He alone can do, we will mess it up every time. We can't save ourselves, nor should we play the role of the Holy Spirit in another person's life. On the other side of the line is our responsibility, which God has clearly shown us in His Word. If we ask God to do what He has told us to do, He won't do it. It isn't because He doesn't want to help us, but because He must stay true to His Word. If God accommodated Himself to every hurting person by changing the way He deals with humanity, He would no longer be God, and His Word could no longer be trusted. People in spiritual conflict cry out to God to protect them, but nothing seems to happen because it is their responsibility to resist the devil, put on the armor of God, stand firm, etc. These people are usually down on themselves and God, and will have to forgive both. God has already provided all we need to get and stay free in Christ.

Determine Beliefs About the Struggle They Are In:

- The origin of their problem
- The nature of their problem
- Spiritual perspective

Note: Many people who are demonically influenced perceive Satan as more powerful, real, and present in their lives than God is. In one poll, 47% of those surveyed have experienced a presence in their room that scared them; 70% have struggled with really bad thoughts or heard voices in the mind like a subconscious self talking to them. They may not be aware that they are spiritually in trouble. Others see themselves as a "freak" -unique or different from other people. Some will not want to part with their "uniqueness;" they may even think what they are experiencing is from God. Still others report that opposing voices sometimes tell them that they will be punished or killed.

Maintain Control by Working Only with the Person

Preliminary considerations:

- Determine as much about the person as you can before you make any attempt at resolution.

- Deception is Satan's primary strategy, but if the demonic is confronted prematurely or irresponsibly, the victim may:

    - become exceedingly distracted or try to leave the room

    - experience internal interference (dizzy, glassy-eyed)

    - receive, but be unable to respond

    - become Catatonic (unable to receive or respond)

Getting their cooperation

In extreme cases, the above can potentially happen even in the best settings conducted by the best pastors/counselors. The goal is to avoid losing control. Since the mind is the control center, the disciple/counselee must cooperate with you by sharing what is going on inside. Satan's deception and lies cannot work without their cooperation. So they must not believe the lies but maintain control over their thought life. It is very important that they agree to share what thoughts they are having in opposition to what you are doing during the session. As soon as the thoughts are revealed, the power of the lie is broken. There are two reasons people may be reticent to share their thoughts with you:

- They're afraid that you won't believe them.

- They are being intimidated.

Usually, it is a threat that they will be thrashed when they get home, or of harm to others if they get free. Getting it out in the open is what maintains control. Satan does everything in the dark because he is the prince of darkness.

Jesus does everything in the light because He is the Light of the world.

The following prayer or something like it is suggested at the beginning of the session:

Dear Heavenly Father, we know that you are here in this room and present in our lives. You are the only all-knowing, all-powerful, ever-present God. We desperately need You because without Jesus we can do nothing. We believe the Bible because it tells us what is really true. We refuse to believe the lies of Satan. We stand in the truth that all authority in heaven and on earth has been given to the resurrected Christ. Because we are in Christ, we share that authority in order to make followers of Jesus and set captives free. We ask You to protect our thoughts and minds, fill us with Your Holy Spirit, and lead us into all truth. We pray for Your complete protection. In Jesus' name, Amen.

Binding is not all-encompassing or absolute.

What to do if there is strong interference.

Personal Time Through the EPIC Journey

As small group leaders or pastors, we cannot take our disciples anywhere we have not gone personally. You will want to personally go through *The Steps to Freedom in Christ* or *EPIC Journey-The Lord's Prayer Journey* before you begin counseling with someone, and utilize these tools regularly.

The Steps to Freedom and the *EPIC Journey* are tools, not the deliverer. Jesus is the real bondage breaker. Whether going through one of these yourself or leading a counselee, we don't just process these truths academically. We are not only interacting with a Biblical tool, but with a personal God who uses His Word to set us free. Don't rush! Give Jesus all the time He wants.

The "Steps to Freedom in Christ"

Counterfeit vs. Real: Renounce non-Christian experiences.

Deception vs. Truth: Where have you been deceived?

Bitterness vs. Forgiveness: Who do you need to forgive?

Rebellion vs. Submission: Replace any rebelliousness with submission.

Pride vs. Humility: In what way are you playing God?

Bondage vs. Freedom: Confess sin to walk in freedom.

Curses vs. Blessings: Renounce generational sin patterns.

The EPIC Journey-The Lord's Prayer Journey

You have an Abba Father – "Our Father in Heaven"

The proper worship of God – "Hallowed be Your Name"

Seeking God's Guidance – "Your Kingdom Come"

Yielding to God's plans — "Your will be done on earth as it is in heaven"

Your provision in Christ – "Give us today our daily bread"

Claiming freedom from sin and bondage — "Forgive us our debts"

Forgiving those who hurt you — "As we forgive our debtors"

Claiming your victory in Christ – "And lead us not into temptation"

Claiming your protection in Christ – "But deliver us from the evil one"

Benediction – "For Yours is the kingdom, and the power and glory forever. Amen"

What if freedom is not obtained?

- You may not have all the necessary information.

- A foundational understanding of their identity in Christ may not be well-established; the "knowing" may not have become the "being" yet.

- False identity equations may still be in operation and need to be renounced and turned from.

- The Lord may be dealing with a few essential layers of bondage; rather than all that needs to be dealt with so as not to overwhelm the person.

- Have them pray, asking the Holy Spirit to reveal what is keeping them in bondage.

Identity-Based Spiritual Formation Terms

Identity-Based Spiritual Formation is a grace-driven, position-in-Christ oriented development process in which the soul grows in conformity to the image of Christ. This process seeks to balance all the needed spiritual approaches.

Positional Spirituality

Positional Spirituality is an approach to the spiritual life that is based on a believer's position or identity in Christ. Identification with Christ in His crucifixion and resurrection (Romans 6:4, Galatians 2:20 and Colossians 3:4) means that our old life has been exchanged for the life of Christ. This approach moves from a works orientation to grace orientation and from legalism to liberty because it centers on our understanding and internalization that Christ's life is our life.

Spirit Filled Spirituality

Spirit-filled Spirituality is an approach that considers how to appropriate the leading and guidance of the Holy Spirit. The believer draws from the Spirit's love, wisdom, and power to live the spiritual life. This approach stresses the biblical implications of the Holy Spirit as a personal being and presence rather than as a mere force.

Process Spirituality

Process Spirituality considers what it means to be faithful to the process of life in Christ rather than being drivel by perceived spiritual "successes" or "failures." It also focuses on abiding in Christ and practicing his presence. In our culture, we increasingly tend to be human "doings" rather than human "beings." The world tells us that what we achieve and accomplish determines who we are, but the Scriptures teach that who we are in Christ should be the basis for what we do. The dynamics of growth are inside out rather than outside in.

Disciplined Spirituality

Disciplined Spirituality stresses the benefits of these varied disciplines. There has been a resurgence of interest in the classical disciplines of the spiritual life. At the same time, it recognizes the needed balance between radical dependence on God and personal discipline as an expression of obedience and application.

Nature

Biblically the word, "nature" is only used twice. Ephesians 2:3 says, "we were by nature children of wrath," and 2 Peter 1:4 says that through the promises of God, we "become partakers of the divine nature, having escaped the corruption that is in the world by lust." Ephesians 5:8 talks about this change in "nature" - "you were formerly darkness, but now you are light in the Lord, walk as children of light." The problem is in the walk. The natural man has a sin nature because he is separated from God.

Does the new creation in Christ retain a sin nature? The difficulty lies in blending together the terms "nature," "old man," and "flesh." The fact that regeneration brings the nature of God into our union with Him is fundamental to a Christian's identity and spiritual maturity. Does the Bible refer to the child of God as a sinner or a saint?

Old man (old self)

This term refers to who the unbeliever is in Adam. First Corinthians 2:14 calls such a person a "natural man" who does not accept the things of God's Spirit but considers them foolishness. Further, it declares that he cannot understand them because such a person is without spiritual discernment. He cannot please God (Romans 8:8).

Scripture declares that in the Christian "our old self was crucified with Christ" (Romans 6:6) so that the authority of sin in the Christian might be rendered powerless. The old self was "in Adam" and under the bondage of sin. The new self is "in Christ." "Therefore if any man is in Christ he is a new creature; the old things passed away, behold new things have come" (2 Corinthians 5:17). It is extremely important to note the tense of the Greek verbs, especially in Romans 6, which is always past tense in relation to the old self and our identity with Christ in His crucifixion. It is important to look at three other passages that mention crucifixion.

Paul declares, "I have been crucified with Christ..." (Galatians 2:20). This is an explanation of Paul's being dead to the law and no longer held by its demands. It came about through his identification in Christ's death and, therefore, is aligned with Romans 6:6.

In Galatians 6:14, Paul disclaims any right to boast "except in the cross of our Lord Jesus Christ, through which the world has been crucified to me and I to the world." This crucifixion of the world is, notice, "to me," and I am crucified "to the world." This refers to the effect of Paul's having been crucified in order to accomplish spiritual liberation as related to the world.

In practical terms for the Christian, the world is crucified "to me, and I to the world" means that love for the world is not something to which we must succumb in our daily experience. This attachment is canceled by the crucifixion of the old self with Christ. This oneness with Christ declares, by means of the apostle Paul's testimony, that the Christians can have an inner disassociation from the world, its values, it's allurements, and its cares. This disassociation does not mean snobbery nor aloofness. Jesus was never guilty of these. In fact, He was so much in the ordinary world that the religious people of His day called Him a glutton and a wine-bibber. But He was inwardly disconnected from the world all the time.

It might be said that:

In Romans 6:6 self is crucified "to sin"

In Galatians 2:20 self is crucified "to the law"

In Galatians 6:14 self if crucified "to the world"

Galatians 5:24 states that those who belong to Christ Jesus have crucified the flesh with its passions and desires. Here, the crucifying of the flesh is stated as being done by the Christian. In none of the preceding passages, is this the case because the crucifying is an accomplished action completed by Christ through the Atonement. The Christian's responsibility to "crucify the flesh" will be dealt with below under the discussion of the term "flesh."

Flesh

This term speaks of the tendency within the soul to center one's interests on self. An unsaved person functions "in the flesh" (Rom. 8:8), worshipping and serving the creature rather than the Creator (Romans 1: 25). In the final analysis, such persons "live for themselves" (2 Corinthians 5:15), even though much of what they do may have an appearance of selflessness and concern for others.

Since the fall, every person is born physically alive but spiritually dead. The unregenerate person learns how to live his life independent of God. It is this learned independence that makes the flesh hostile to God. Self-serving, self-justifying survival techniques, known as defense mechanisms, are what characterize the flesh. The flesh serves self. It became the channel of sinful actions through the fall (Genesis 3). Satan made his appeal to Eve concerning the forbidden tree on the basis of the three channels mentioned in 1 John 2:16:

The lust of the flesh.   The lust of the eyes.   The boastful pride of life.

Genesis 3:6 describes this appeal to which Eve responded. The "explanation" for her decision to act in disobedience to God is given in three descriptive phrases. Notice the response when the woman saw that the tree was:

"good for food" (the lust of the flesh)
"delight to the eyes" (the lust of the eyes)
"desirable to make one wise" (the boastful pride of life)

What was there in Eve to which these appeals were made? What in her responded to them? It was not her "old self" or "old man" (Romans 6:6), for, at that point, she had no "old self," not having yet sinned. Sin had not yet entered into the world (Romans 5:12).

Satan appealed to her "flesh," that capability of the soul to act in one's own behalf, to serve self. The advent of sin in the world changed everything.

The flesh was perverted into selfishness. The flesh now exists in opposition to God. For this reason, we are told that *"the mind that is set on the flesh is hostile toward God; for it does not subject itself to the law of God, for it is not even able to do so"* (Romans. 8:7).

The Corinthians were rebuked for being "carnal" (KJV) or "fleshly" (NASB) in I Corinthians 3:1-3. This characteristic is shown in spiritual childishness, jealousy, strife, division, and misplaced identities (e.g., some were identifying with Paul or Apollos or Cephas instead of with Christ (see also I Corinthians 1:11-13; 3:22-23). Scripture uses two forms of referring to persons in relation to the flesh. One is "those who are in the flesh" (Romans 7:5; 8:8-9). Clearly, one who is "in" the flesh is not a Christian. Those who are "in the Spirit" are those in whom the Spirit of God dwells. Without this, one does not belong to God (Romans 8:9-11) nor understand the things of God (I Corinthians 1:12-13). The second is "after the flesh" (KJV) or "according to the flesh" (NASV). This terminology is used in Romans 7 and 8, I Corinthians 3, Galatians 5, etc., and refers to living according to our previously learned independence. It is possible for a Christian to fall into actions or reactions that are sinful and thus walk (or live) "according to the flesh." The deeds of the flesh (the demonstrations of fleshly living) are evident, says Paul, and he lists them in Galatians 5:19-21.

What makes this possible is that our old self *was* crucified with Christ. God changed our basic nature in regeneration; it is our responsibility to change our behavior. Christian growth (the process of sanctification) is predicated on the complete and perfect work of the atonement; crucifying the "old self" and uniting the believer in Christ (2 Corinthians 5:21). The Christian, complete in Christ (Colossians 2:10) and enabled by the Holy Spirit to understand his true identity in Christ, must choose to walk by the Spirit and believe that which God has said is true. The Christian begins to experience what it means to "walk in newness of life" (Romans 6:4) and "serve in newness of the Spirit" (Romans 7:6) as he walks by faith in the power of the Holy Spirit. The problem is in our walk, not our existence or essence.

Sin

Sin is the condition into which all are born as descendants of fallen Adam (Romans 5:12). Sin is fostered by the deception that identity and purpose in life can be achieved apart from a dependent and personal relationship with the Creator (Deuteronomy 30:19-20, I John 5:11-12). It dominates the old self, affecting every part of one's being: the body (Isaiah 1:4-6), the affections (Jeremiah 17:9-10, Romans 1:26-27), the intellect (Ephesians 4:17-18, Romans 1:28), the spirit (Ephesians 2:1-2), the will (Romans 6:16, 2 Peter 2:19), and the emotions (Ephesians 4:19, 2 Timothy 3:1-4).

Sin is more than a principle, for the "one who practices sin is of the devil; for the devil has sinned from the beginning" (1 John. 3:8). When a Christian is set free from the power of sin, he is set free from Satan and the kingdom of darkness. The concept of sin is shown in the following passages.

> *"All unrighteousness is sin"* (1 John 5:17). (Commission of actions known to be wrong in God's sight.)

> *"Therefore, to one who knows the right thing to do, and does not do; to him, it is sin"* (James 4:17). (Omission of action known to be right in God's sight.)

> *"Everyone who practices sin practices lawlessness; and sin is lawlessness"* (1 John 3:4). (Violation of God's stated standard.)

> *"But if you show partiality, you are committing sin"* (James 2:9). (Responding differently to people because of class or racial distinctions.)

> *"But he who doubts is condemned if he eats because his eating is not from faith, and whatever is not from faith is sin"* (Romans 14:23). (Action taken in spite of doubt as to whether what is done is right in God's sight.)

Sin hasn't died, nor is it removed when we receive Christ, but our relationship with sin has ended, and its power to dominate is broken through the believer's crucifixion, resurrection, and righteousness in Christ (Romans 6:7; 12-16; 8:10, I John 3:8). In Romans 7:15-17 and 20, it is explained that when a Christian fails (or sins), it is through response to sin which is "in" the Christian, but is not "the Christian himself."

Because the old self is crucified with Christ, sin need not be served (Romans 6:6-7; 17-18; 20-22). Satan is committed to keeping the non-believer under the penalty of sin by blinding the mind of the unbelieving (2 Corinthians 4:4). When that battle is lost at salvation, he doesn't curl up his tail and pull in his fangs; he now commits himself to keeping the Christian under the power of sin.

New Self (New Man)

This term represents the incredible work of Christ's redemption in the life of the believer. Man's old self is replaced by something that did not exist in him before. He is declared to be a "new creation" (2 Corinthians 5:17, Galatians 6:15). He is now something that he previously was not before. He has become one spirit with the Lord (1 Corinthians 6:17). In the practice of daily living, the Christian is exhorted to "put on the new man" (i.e., by faith to function in the light of one's true identity in Christ - see Ephesians 4:24, Colossians 3:10).

This new man is nothing other than Jesus Christ's life implanted within the believer and manifested in practical ways as the Christian makes moral choices in the power of the Spirit (2 Corinthians 4:10-11, Romans 8:12-13; 13:14). The significance of this truth is the believer's identity. Possessing a new nature—Christ's very nature—we are not "partly new and partly old," nor are we "partly light and partly darkness," but we are a new creature in Him.

Does this mean the believer is sinless? By no means! Sin can continue to dwell in the body and continue to make its appeal. But it does mean that by virtue of the crucifixion of the old man, sin's power is broken (Romans. 6:7,12,14), and the believer is under no obligation to obey or respond to sin. He can, by the grace of God, live as a child of light (Ephesians 5:8-11).

The believer will be under conviction when he chooses to believe the lie, which says that identity and purpose in life can be found in the course of action contrary to and independent of God. Returning to legalism or license brings the believer into bondage again (Romans 6:16, Galatians 5:1, 13). But, when the believer walks according to the flesh, he is violating his true nature (Romans 7:16, 22), and freedom must be regained through repentance (Proverbs 28:13, I John 1:9). Conviction is sensed when we choose to act differently from who we really are in Christ.

Identity in Christ
This term is not used in Scripture, but the concept is taught repeatedly throughout the New Testament. Because human life is lived in accordance with one's perceived identity, this subject is of tremendous importance. No one can consistently behave in a way that is inconsistent with how he views himself.

If Christians are no different inwardly from non-Christians, or if they perceive themselves to be no different, then their lifestyles will be virtually indistinguishable from the lifestyles of non-Christians. Often this results from repeated defeats in the Christian's life. The enemy, Satan, then capitalizes by pouring on guilt, and coupled with the negative emphasis of legalistic teachers, the believer questions his salvation or accepts as normal an up-and-down spiritual existence. The defeated Christian confesses his wretchedness and proneness to sin, strives to do better, but inwardly considers that he is just a sinner saved by grace hanging on until the rapture.

Why does this describe so many Christians? Because of ignorance of one's true identity in Christ. This inner change is effected the moment of salvation; its outer counterpart in the daily walk of the believer continues throughout life. This is the work of "sanctification." But the progressive work of sanctification only has its full and powerful effect in one's life as newness in Christ is realized and appropriated by faith.

We are identified with Him:

   a. In His death (Romans 6:3, 6, Galatians 2:20, Colossians 3:1-3)

   b. In His burial (Romans 6:4)

   c. In His resurrection (Romans 6:5; 8,11)

   d. In His life (Romans 5:10-11)

   e. In His power (Ephesians 1:19-20)

   f. In His inheritance (Romans 8:16-17, Ephesians 1:11-12)

The apostle Paul (through whom all the above identifications are expressed) describes himself in I Timothy 1:15 as the foremost of sinners. However, this statement is made in a context (vv. 12-16), which clearly shows it as a reference to his unsaved condition. He makes a similar statement of self-depreciation in 1 Corinthians 15:9 but follows it in the next breath with "but by the grace of God I am what I am, and His grace toward me did not prove vain" (v. 10). All that is needed for godly living is ours by divine power, which is inherent in the Christ-life within (2 Peter 1:3, Galatians 2:20, Romans 8:37). The believer's identity and purpose are in Christ. He becomes a doer of the word because of who he already is. He does not do to become. Rather, he becomes an obedient doer of the Word as the result of already being one with Christ (James 1:22-25).

In Scripture, believers are called "brethren," "children," "sons of God," "sons of light," "light in the Lord," "saints," not "sinners saved by grace." Why is this the case? Do believers ever sin? Yes, they do. The names given to believers in the Bible correspond to their new identity in Christ. They have died to sin and are now alive in Jesus Christ (Romans 6:11). This new identity in no way gives license to the pretender. It gives power to the authentic believer by means of Christ's indwelling and never-changing life.

If a true Christian believes himself a sinner, then his core identity is sin. This is a direct contradiction to Scripture which states a believer has been justified by faith. If a Christian is a sinner, then what do sinners do? They sin! What would you expect a sinner to do? We are not "sinners saved by grace," but "saints who sin." Sin's power has been broken; the will is now able to choose the truth by the power of the Holy Spirit, and the truth sets one free (John. 8:31-32). He does so when by faith, a believer chooses to "be" what, in reality, he already "is" in Christ.

Basis for Identity – The Image of God

"So God created man in his own image, in the image of God he created him; male and female he created them" (Genesis1:27). When God breathed into man, he became a living being, unique from all other creation. Since God does not exist in the flesh (2 Corinthians 5:16), the image man reflects is not found in physical existence. Man is more than a physical being; he is a spiritual being, a living soul. Unlike the animal kingdom, which functions by divine instinct, man was created with the ability to think, feel, and choose. Before the fall, man was spiritually alive, and he functioned in harmony with God. What sin brought in the fall was spiritual death (separation from God). The immediate effect upon man was that his moral nature was corrupted. The reason Jesus came as the Messiah was to bring a fallen humanity spiritual life and then to change their nature. To present Jesus as someone who will only help meet our psychological needs is to distort the gospel and undermine true Christian counseling. Every cult leader and humanistic self-helper will promise psychological help and will line up their customers to testify on their behalf. Man did not completely lose the image of God in which he was created, or he would have ceased being a man. He spiritually died, his moral nature was corrupted, and the image was severely tarnished, but he continued to think, feel, and choose.

EPIC Events

Our passion at Infusion Ministries is to train pastors and other leaders to help their people understand what it means to be a child of God and walk in freedom from destructive habits. We provide training and resources for all ages and groups. In addition to the summits below, we have training tailored to parents, small group leaders and others. Contact us for more details and how you can join us in Knoxville, TN, for a summit, or bring these powerful truths to your church or ministry. Call (865) 966-1153, or visit infusionnow.org for the most up to date information on our events.

EPIC Summit

This three-day summit is held live in Knoxville, TN, and broadcast on ZOOM in the spring and fall, and consists of three parts:

- **Identity:** EPIC Identity material walks us through the biblical truths about who we are in Christ and how to replace the negative, false ideas we have believed about ourselves with these truths.

- **Freedom:** Satan wants to keep us in bondage to destructive habits, addictions, fear, anger, unforgiveness and more. However, Jesus came to set us free. EPIC Freedom provides tools to win the battle for the mind and live in His freedom.

- **The Lord's Prayer Journey:** We utilize the Lord's Prayer as a means for the Holy Spirit to reveal any doors opened to the enemy, unresolved spiritual conflict or unforgiveness and help us claim freedom.

EPIC Leadership Summits

This two-day summit is held live and broadcast via ZOOM in Knoxville, TN, once a year.

- **EPIC Leader I:** So many leaders do not feel qualified or equipped to help those with spiritual conflicts and bondage. EPIC Leader I provides biblical tools and principles that will help you bring the message of identity and freedom in Christ to your church or organization.

- **EPIC Leader II:** Provides material that will give you a clear model and guide to discipleship counseling and tools to help all believers overcome their spiritual conflicts.

EPIC Latino Summit

This is a five-day summit, held live in Knoxville, TN, once a year in late summer, and may be broadcast on ZOOM. EPIC Identity, Freedom and Journey are combined with EPIC Leadership 1 and Leadership 2 materials - all presented in Spanish. Contact us for information on the next EPIC Latino Summit.

EPIC Christian Adventures

This outdoor camp experience for men is to help them discover their true identity and freedom in Christ so they can live as the men God has made them to be. You will enjoy excellent meals, hiking and fishing and the opportunity to encounter God without the distractions of daily life. To learn about our next adventure, call Infusion Ministries at 865-966-1153 or visit infusionnow.org.

The Holy Land Tour, led by Dr. Dave Park

During this life-altering journey, usually in June, we tour numerous natural, civic and religious sites described in scriptures and share in meaningful times of worship, instruction, and prayer. To find out more information about the next trip, visit our website at **infusionnow.org**.

Made in the USA
Columbia, SC
19 January 2021